HONORABLE DISCHARGES:
Basic Training Children Need to Own Before They Leave Home

by

Helen Ryan Miles

DORRANCE PUBLISHING CO
EST. 1920
PITTSBURGH, PENNSYLVANIA 15238

Dorrance Publishing Co
585 Alpha Drive
Pittsburgh, PA 15238
Visit our website at *www.dorrancebookstore.com*

ISBN: 978-1-6366-1174-7
eISBN: 978-1-6366-1765-7

Ryan tapestry on cover created in honor of our parents
50th Wedding anniversary (1997)
by daughter, Laura.

INTRODUCTION

I have toyed with this idea long enough. Truth is, my parents were geniuses. In my estimation, they tried with all due diligence to instill practical wisdoms and precepts for living which would enhance ours and others lives for generations to come. Much of their teaching originated from the school of common sense, the academy of manners and etiquette and the college of more qualitative, more consequential and more significant living. They would never give themselves this much if any credit for the quality of the "fruit" nurtured on their watch. So I will. "Phenomenal job, Mom and Pops"!

I do not have children nor have I had the awesome privilege or responsibility for raising any. I do know what it's like to be parented and parented well. I know what it feels like to be nurtured, affirmed and valued. I never heard our parents jesting with anyone (as I have heard some parents do) about whether they'd like to "take us for the week-end" (or longer) just to get us out of their hair. They never seemed to be in a hurry for us to grow up and get out; in fact sometimes I wondered if they ever really wanted us to leave at all. There were probably many private moments when one or both parents wished for a break from all they had on their plates including six energetic, inquisitive and ever- challenging children but we never heard them express it.

My father had a slightly different view regarding the 'never wanting us to leave home' spiel; while he did love us, his love seemed much less accommodating or should I say, forgiving. I guess you could describe it as a "tougher" kind of love. Mom used to say that if any one of us kids had an issue with the rules of the house, we could leave when we turned eighteen. Pops simply declared that we could leave "now"! I once asked my mother when she most worried about us and her very prompt response was, "when you weren't with me". Not that she knew it all including having all the answers for our multitude of woes but somewhere deep within, her ardent desire to keep us safe and sound was best rendered (she believed) under her watchful eye alone. She knew she couldn't be everywhere but as much and as often as was motherly possible, she wanted to be.

Mom thought it her solemn duty to "snoopervise" us as situations warranted. I don't believe my father fretted as much when we were not under their watchful guidance. He just expected us to behave the way in which we were taught and use our "common sense" to solve problems or to get out of a jam. Again, much less forgiving, he often bellowed, "Why were you there in the first place?" or any other fitting interrogative.

I mentioned earlier that I never had children. However, I taught or worked with them in our county school district for 34 years. In 1978, the beginning of my teaching career, it was much easier to deliver words of traditional and "tried and true" wisdom in contrast to the latter years. By the late nineties and 2000's, there was a most blatant and palpable change in the manner in which children responded to admonitions that I deemed constructive criticisms or simple correction. You were often "yelling" (as they viewed it) or picking on them almost to the point where you were less inclined about saying

anything at all. But that's another book.

What a privilege it is now for me to share some of the practical wisdoms our parents taught us. And by the way, you will see me use "my" and "our" interchangeably when referring to my parents. You will also notice my use of Dad or "Pops" when referring to my father. They raised six phenomenal children and the lessons learned impacted us often-times similarly, many times differently, and most of all, certainly. I hope that what is shared with you, will encourage you to add to your repertoire of lessons imparted to your own unique and wonderful children.

BOOK REVIEWS FOR HONORABLE DISCHARGES

Honorable Discharges is a fabulous historical journey of African-American life from the turn of the century to today. It is the story of an honorable middle class family in Central Florida that prepared their children to be successful members of the community while following a strong spiritual foundation and solid values not only in Daytona Beach, but globally.

William and Nettie Ryan were strict but loving parents. Mr. Ryan served in World War II and Mrs. Ryan also served her country and later became an educator.

The Ryan family reminded me so much of my own as they provided rich culture and experiences that most did not have. From high educational standards to proper etiquette and respect for others .This book is definitely a page turner and highly recommended.

I will never forget this book and the many lessons encompassed within its covers.

Davita B. Bonner
Roots Revisited Book Club

*   *   *

A well-crafted story about family and the deep roots the family has in the Daytona Beach area. I am in awe of all of the etiquette points that are not used today that were pointed out in the story. And, it would be great if those sections could be pulled out in a booklet entitled "Common Courtesy Counts." This book has great historical significance in the history of Daytona Beach. Most families have gaps in their religious teachings and acceptances, but all of us with some rooted understanding will always say "God's grace is sufficient and I am glad I have some."

Kenneth Hunt, MBA
Director
Office of Diversity and Inclusion
Embry-Riddle Aeronautical University
Florida/Arizona/ Worldwide

*   *   *

This book is an easy read about an extraordinary couple with humble beginnings who raised successful well-rounded children in a complex world. Helen Ryan Miles navigates the reader through some lessons learned from her parents. She methodically lays out a plan to assist today's parents with basic child-rearing drawn from the lessons learned. This book will become one of your favorite resources on child-rearing.

Vivian Lee, M.Ed, Ed.S
(Retired High School Counselor)

*   *   *

Honorable Discharges by Helen Ryan Miles is an engaging, easy to read, yet powerful book that demonstrates the importance of training children at home. Helen uses short stories about her parents that demonstrate how they played a critical role in shaping she and her sibling's thoughts, actions and their values which equipped them for a successful and joyful life beyond their home. This book inspires you to embrace the forgotten basic tenet of "home training." I believe this book can be a vital tool for equipping parents to ensure the next generation's future is bright. I love the "Questions for the Round Table". These can be used with your family and friends, a parents' group, or a small church group. It gets a 5-star rating!

Patricia Larkins Hicks, Ph.D.
President, Outcomes Management Group, LTD
Columbus, OH

*   *   *

An ode to family and parenthood. A recital of loving, learning, and living. A vital pattern woven into the tapestry of the black family evolution. The need for parent to discipline til their children are able to discipline themselves(as Jesus did his disciples, from which the word "discipline" comes). The spiritual growth, the "mothers wit ," the study materials contained here comprises an entertaining and educational experience for all readers. Well done, Helen!

Julius Bennett

DEDICATION

This book is dedicated to the memory of my parents, William and Nettie Ryan, whose love and support was unfailing, unconditional, and to this day, a sustaining and guiding force in my life.

Mom and "Pops," I cherish the memory of the times that your hearts "sang" with joy and gladness. Forgive me however, for the times when I failed or disappointed you. I realized later and even more fully now what jewels of parents you were, and I love you to life for having been the God-given vessel by which I came to be and the perfect gifts you still are to me.

Your Grateful Daughter,
Helen

I consider it right, as long as I live in this body, to stir you up by reminding you, knowing that soon I will take off this body, even as our Lord Jesus Christ has shown me. And I will also be diligent to make sure that after my death you will always remember these things.   2 Peter 1: 13-15

Preface:

Let me tell you what this book is not; it is not autobiographical in the sense that my life story and those of my siblings will be told in this narrative, and it is not a memoir by any stretch of the imagination. It is not even an attempt to document examples of how these lessons helped contribute to our success if you will. It is not about the virtues of courage, determination, perseverance under pressure, and countless other merits, although we did learn these and other values both directly and indirectly. It is, however, an attempt to share some of the more practical wisdoms, which in addition to the more philosophical lessons, provided us more of a "cutting edge" on the road to more qualitative living. Ultimately readers will glean for themselves why these peculiar "little but big things" were so important to our parents.

I submit that perhaps some or much of what we were taught might not ever have occurred to legions of well-meaning and loving parents. Raising children is a gargantuan responsibility; this declaration is not born of personal experience because I have none. However, I have seen what good parenting looks like, up close and personal. I said good parenting, not perfect parenting. My mother often declared that "if I had to do it all over again, I would or wouldn't…" (Whatever the case may have been). Many of the lessons we were taught have indeed served us well by opening doors of opportunities to experiences we may never have had or by having others view us more favorably because of them. They might "strike a familiar chord" with some, be a little extraneous or unnecessary to others, and apropos for many. Mama wanted others to think well of us. Period.

A Lesson from Our Father

My father always declared that, "If you lie, you'll steal," a position from which he never wavered. He expected a truthful response when queried as to whether we had or had not done or said something we should or should not have. He believed that honesty was tied to trust; it was a gage of one's character. If one was not truthful, how could he be trusted? He grew up in an era when a man's word was his bond. Contracts laden with often unfathomable language were not always necessary; instead a firm handshake often sealed many a deal.

Good character included honoring your commitments, or else no one who knew you would ever dare do business with you again. It was over, and you were proverbially finished. Who wants to live the rest of his life in a dark hole of mistrust and disdain? Every move subject to suspicion and scrutiny the likes of which you have never seen.

As we matured and life happened, as they say, truth became much more complicated than a simple "yes or "no" response to a straightforward question. Truth is still truth, no doubt, but life's complicated, and we learn how to "handle" the truth with more grace and more love, especially if we are the ones having to be truthful with others or if we're on the receiving end of a loving, graceful, and sometimes brutal chastening.

Lies must be nurtured to the point of exhaustion; there is no way to remember all the details of its many "faces": Death, destruction, mayhem, confusion, broken relationships, and mistrust are lies' ill-fated offspring.

The Ryan children lied but probably no more or less than any other children. We had a heavy-handed father who did not believe in sparing the rod. He believed it to be the swiftest, surest method of correction. Sometimes lying (when we thought we could get away with it) was the only way to avoid the wrath of our dad, for his temper was as heavy as the hands used to mete out punishment. It was always better to be truthful from the beginning. Sometimes we were spared the rod when we did. Thank goodness the spankings, though severe, were relatively infrequent. My siblings may differ with me on this one.

Don't lie. Take it from a man who grew up during the Great Depression, whose family made difficult but necessary choices to survive and live decently and honorably. A man who is considered to be, according to journalist Tom Brokaw, a part of "the greatest generation" serving gallantly during WWII in the Pacific Theater. He later married my mom, she, too, a veteran of WWII. He fathered six children and moved on to become a successful contributor to his community and society at large.

The truth, though liberating, exhilarating, and refreshing, can be equally as terrifying, restrictive, and hurtful. It is most probably better to tell the truth the first time out. And if honesty is truly the best policy, remember that an ounce of tenderness coupled with forgiveness makes truth more palatable, especially when we need to be truthful with others, or as alluded to earlier when we are the recipient of tough, truthful love. Some level of punishment or fall-out my still be your lot, but you've got to jump into the ocean of truth and pray that the sea of forgiveness throws you a life raft.

BE GENEROUS WITH YOUR COMPLIMENTS

Mama used to say that "it doesn't take anything away from you to be nice to people or to pay them a sincere compliment." Some people believe though that paying a compliment or speaking favorably about someone else elevates that person above themselves. It practically "kills" some people to extend a compliment; heaven forbid they're in a situation where the general consensus favors someone and they're "forced" to go along with it, so as not to appear jealous or snobbish.

A compliment is the easiest thing to pay (just made that up). But there are people who just can't seem to "pay" one to save their skin, even to the point of discomfort when others are complimentary. This hesitancy or refusal may be driven by selfishness or jealousy, but I believe that fear is the root here. Yes, fear. The fear that other people may appear to be valued above them. The fear that others may achieve or acquire more than they. Or the fear, as aforementioned, that it somehow diminishes them. Of course if one's self-esteem is already fragile, the fear of further damage to one's own.

Perhaps no one ever paid attention to them or recognized their value. Often people are dissatisfied with their station in life, especially if they have failed to reach desired goals or if they have not achieved at a level they feel acceptable.

Disappointments litter the paths of some more than others, but the extent to which negativity has marred their entire outlook on life is both exasperating and mysterious. Some never seem to recognize, let alone embrace what appears to others to be the obvious good, the obvious beauty, and the obvious human need to show compassion in times of need. Their apparent self-absorption spills over into many areas of theirs as well as the lives of others. My impatience with this level of negativity prompted Mama to remind me on one occasion that often "they just don't have anybody to encourage them," and in so many instances, she was absolutely on target. I cannot name all of the people who shared the many ways in which Mom encouraged, comforted, provided refuge, and simply listened to them through the years; their names are legion.

Negative, bitter, and selfish people are some of the most difficult to embrace, but we must, simply because they need it most. Don't deprive others of that good word most probably yearned for all day, all week, all month, all year, or even perhaps all of their lives. A caveat; be careful not to patronize or behave as if you're doing them a favor, as this is one of the highest forms of insincerity. A good word of praise or recognition spoken with the best of intentions and the purest of heart can soften even the hardest of hearts and positively affect someone's world for a lifetime.

I found these notes amongst Mom's papers after her passing. She recorded them on December 4th, 2014 from a television broadcast.

Don't miss opportunities to be nice to people.
Pour in (or) on Honor to people
Be generous with your compliments!
Pour on some oil of Honor!

Just Who Were "Nick" and Nettie

On the surface, my parents are the perfect example of polar opposites in terms of demeanor, interests, vision, and philosophy. One might wonder how two totally different individuals would find what had to have been common ground in order for the "twain" to meet.

On the other hand, having known one another from childhood, attending the same schools and serving in the military at a crucial and consequential time in our nation's history provided a great foundation for cultivating a friendship and launching a "loveship," which eventually culminated in marriage. To my father's credit, he instinctively knew the kind of woman his future children would come to love, honor, respect, and proudly call "Mama." It didn't hurt that Mom had the prettiest legs in town either. Brilliant selection, Dad! And though he was not always emotionally demonstrative when it came to heart issues, Mom once shared with me that she always appreciated his long-held affinity for her grandpa and the care extended him during a brief stay with them until his passing.

My father was pretty good at sizing up people without taking "all day;" he could detect a lying spirit, a haughty manner, evil intent, or inherent goodness. (By the way, his mother called him "Nick" not knowing that "Bill" is the nickname for William, my dad's real name). If he liked you or believed you liked him, he could and would engage in lively conversation, but he was usually slow to speak unless provoked or if something was sparked in conversation which captured his interest. He could be opinionated but often bordered on the taciturn. In other words, he knew when to keep his mouth shut.

He once feuded with one of our mayors until sidewalks were installed on our street. Of course he had to initiate a petition requiring signatures from all of our neighbors. Needless to say, his persistence paid off, and the engineers began drawing up plans for those long-overdue sidewalks on Desoto Street! A male chauvinist of sorts, I think he was "testing" our no-nonsense female mayor to determine whether she would make good on the project, and of course, she did!

But there was one thing he would not tolerate and that was disrespectful behavior aimed at him or our mom. He swiftly defended himself against all enemies, "foreign or domestic," and he definitely defended Mom if anyone disrespected her, especially us kids.

Dad enjoyed sports; he ran track as a student at Kentucky State College. We remember his love of professional boxing, baseball, basketball, football, and golf, especially with the introduction of Tiger Woods. He loved supporting the Dodgers, Chiefs, Pirates, Cavaliers, Joe Louis, Muhammed Ali, LeBron James, and selected other teams and athletes. He also loved employing his "green thumb" for planting and cultivating flowers, plants, and fruit trees. His "softer" and more artistic side really shined when outside amongst the plants, flowers, and shrubbery in our award-winning lawn.

When I gaze at the pictures of my parents in uniform, I marvel at just how young they were as soldiers and enlistees during the Second World War; Dad enlisted at the age of twenty and Mom at age eighteen. They looked so mature and so distinguished in their uniforms, fighting to defend a not so grateful nation against the evils of Fascism, Nazism, and Imperialistic Japan. It seems almost unfathomable that human beings so young would be charged with the responsibility of defending a nation against threats of this magnitude and with such dire consequences. But like so many of their generation who answered the call, or who as in Mom's case, volunteered for service, they considered it an honor and their patriotic duty. For six months prior to his entry into the service, Dad was employed by American Brand Textile Company in Wallington, New Jersey. There he operated a weaving machine, which made rugs, curtains, and hair nets.

My father served in the South Pacific Theater: New Guinea, the Philippines, and New Britain Island as a radar operator with the 742nd

AAA artillery gun battalion. He fought in the Bismarck Archipelago Campaign. Mom served stateside at Fort Huachuca near Phoenix, AZ and Des Moines, Iowa among others. Reticent about sharing their experiences, but when they did, it was always with pride and humility. Mom one time joked that the older enlistees sort of looked after her because she was one of the youngest. She graduated from the clerk's course in Des Moines, Iowa, January 1945, and dental tech school November 1945. Both honorably discharged, they eventually made their way back home to Fort Myers, marrying in 1947, then on to Kentucky State College where Dad enrolled in the shoe repair program and Mom pursued her Bachelor's degree.

Family illness brought my parents back to Fort Myers and eventually Daytona Beach, where Mom completed her degree in the Social Sciences and Dad enrolled in the tailoring program at Bethune-Cookman College. He later worked a variety of jobs, including bell hop, custodian, and produce manager at the local Food Fair grocery store, a job he truly enjoyed as it allowed him the freedom and creativity necessary to assess the integrity of fruit and vegetables and to display them in a manner enticing to the buyer. Occasionally my brothers helped him on Saturday evenings during inventory.

Between life in Frankfurt, Kentucky and Daytona, six children were born to their union; my siblings Homer, Alfred, Charles, Patricia, and Laura; I was number four and the first girl.

Mom had a way with others that made them feel special. She was brilliant, articulate, warm, welcoming, and insightful. Taking her role as mother seriously, she never failed to exercise that inalienable right until her last breath, irrespective of our ages.

She loved entertaining small groups on special occasions as well as casual get togethers. Often Mom moved about the house humming a familiar or not so familiar show tune, spiritual, or popular song. One of her favorite entertainers was Tina Turner, who happened to own a dynamite pair of legs like Mom's. I remember when she attended one of her concerts while on tour in Orlando. Mom admired her for her "gutsiness" in leaving the popular rock duo known as Ike and Tina Turner to further her career as a solo act. She looked like a rock star that night, herself! In addition to entertaining, she had a penchant for collecting stamps, coins, and a decades-long archive of interesting articles from various print media.

Mom volunteered her services in the civic, religious, and social arenas serving on the boards of community development, the library, and the rape crisis center task force. Her volunteerism also included working with the juvenile court, public schools, political campaigns, and Sigma Gamma Rho Sorority (one of the Divine Nine). She also wrote a column for our local black newspaper, the "Daytona Times"; all of this in addition to owning and operating a child care business after retiring from the public school system as teacher and librarian.

Yes, Nick and Nettie were unique in their own right, but the one thing they shared was a burning desire to raise children who could care for themselves, would care about others, and leave where ever they had been better than when they found it. That said I know they loved us and believed in their hearts that when their work was finished, they could rest assured that their children merited the distinction of having been honorably discharged into a world awaiting their time, their God-given talent and their resources.

NURTURE A HEALTHY RESPECT FOR EDUCATION AND LEARNING IN GENERAL

Michael Bloomberg, former Mayor of New York City said on January 17th, 2008 that *"college isn't for everyone, but education is."*

My mother in particular nurtured a healthy respect for education and an appreciation for learning. Whether we were learning how to hem a skirt or a pair of pants, wash the dishes, memorize a poem, change a tire, hang a picture, prune a flower, or write a thank you letter, "All learning has merit and all work is honorable," she said.

Learning, the way my mother defined it, was not limited to the experiences and the knowledge gleaned behind the walls of ivy at schools of academia; it also included those lessons learned by using our hands, calling upon our innate creativity, and exercising our God-given talent. Ultimately a "wedding" of the aesthetic, academic, technical, and vocational would better serve ourselves and others.

She was passionate, almost to a fault (some maintained), about the benefits of a good education. This passion most probably took root as a very young woman.

Her mother, Helen Verona Cox Hawkins Goodman, earned her junior college diploma from Bethune-Cookman College on July 22nd,

1939. Just a few years later, Helen signed a contract with the Glades County Board of Public Instruction where she accepted an assignment to teach at the George Washington School for coloreds (not capitalized on her contract) in the city of Moore Haven, Florida. Moore Haven, a little town in the southwestern part of the state near Fort Myers, is known for its rich soil, famously called the "muck," perfect for growing the sweetest produce you've ever eaten, particularly sugar cane, melons, mango, citrus, and corn. The area is also known for its fresh water fishing straight out of Lake Okeechobee, the largest in Florida, and a lifeline to other cities in the region, such as Clewiston, LaBelle, and Pahokee. My grandmother attained prominence in the city of Moore Haven not because she was a teacher but because she was a darn good one. Her compassion for others and dedication to her craft were well-known.

My youngest sister and I accompanied our parents to a school reunion at what is now a middle/high school there in Moore Haven. This new building was the apparent "successor" to the school where Grandma Helen taught and over which she once presided. It was in the late eighties or early nineties when we made this most historic and eye-opening trip. Needless to say, what we were destined to learn would help us to "connect the dots" with regard to Mom's passion for learning in general and for education in particular.

We mingled amongst the people who once attended the one-room school house and who remembered Grandma when they were children. I shall never forget the sentiments of one woman regarding the commitment of Grandma Helen to teaching and learning. She declared unequivocally that "there was no such thing as 'Johnny can't read' with Miss Helen. She made sure that everyone learned how to read."

The pride in my mother's heart illuminated her face as the glowing testimonies poured out about her precious mother, who had died in her early forties leaving her daughter, Nettie (my mother), who was exactly twenty years her junior. My sister and I were equally proud to hear those words spoken about a grandmother we never knew and for whom I was named. This interchange provided me additional insight about Mom's commitment to education and the extent to which her mother's values were transformative for her and other families in the community where Grandma served.

My grandmother declared on her sick bed that she could not die until her only child, Nettie, earned her college degree. Mom wanted more than anything to remain with her mother for the duration of her illness, but Grandmother insisted she return to Kentucky State College in Frankfort, Kentucky to finish her freshman and sophomore years. After Grandma's passing, Mom decided to remain in state and complete her education closer to home by earning her B.S. in Secondary Education from Bethune-Cookman College on August 9th, 1952 – still honoring her dying mother's wishes. She majored in the social sciences with certifications in English and library science. Over the years, Mom realized what her mother always knew that earning her formal education was not so much for her mother Helen's benefit but for her own.

It has been my distinct honor over the years to hear testimonies of my mother's compassion and concern for her students and for people in general. Her students swore that "Nettie Ryan" was amongst a dying breed of teachers who took your problems home with them, who taught earnestly, loved toughly, and yet made you feel special at the same time. She ardently defended and protected the art of teaching, and finally from her mother, embraced the truth that planting good seeds early in your children might very well result in new generations of children who are eager to learn and who will come to appreciate the benefits of education, be it technical, academic, vocational, or by way of sage advice and common sense handed down through the generations.

Reading and the Aesthetics

In addition to the academics, Mom was equally enthusiastic about aesthetics (beauty and the arts). Undoubtedly she was born with a keen sense of beauty and a strong interest in the culture of her community and that of the world. Perhaps that is what drew her to major in social studies and geography. Mom's beloved grandfather, Homer Cox, was active in the civic and religious life of their Fort Myers community. In fact he was instrumental in acquiring the first charter for an NAACP branch there in 1939. Some thirty-seven to thirty-eight years later, yours truly became a charter member of the NAACP on the campus of Florida State University in Tallahassee, Florida. Well there you have it, love for the community was in her DNA and in mine as well. She thrived on interchanges revolving around world events and lit up at just the thought of people, places, and things and how they shaped unique world communities. Mom never traveled the world, but you wouldn't know it by the way her conversations were often replete with references encompassing all points of the globe.

I clearly remember the title of one of her seventh-grade social studies teacher's edition text, *A World View*. Apropos in terms of what she tried to instill in her students and in us, her children.

Sometimes, in her exasperation with our apparent lack of interest in anything or our resistance to "sound" instruction, she'd say, "I'm not raising you just for us (referring to our parents). I'm raising you for the world." She desperately wanted us to broaden our horizons and look beyond our immediate surroundings with an eye on and for the global community.

Our parents did all they were able to do to expose us to as much as our community and beyond had to offer. They took my three older brothers to our nation's capital, and when we were older, me and my two younger sisters. They wanted us to experience the ebb and flow of the seat of our government, view the sights, visit the museums, and other places of interest. One of my fondest memories was of visiting the White House around the age of thirteen. It was breath-taking to share the excitement with people from the world over anxiously waiting to inhale the warmth and splendor of our first family's home. Adding to my excitement, we glimpsed a leader from one of the African nations motorcading away from the White House in a black limousine of course. Closer to home, the theater, the opera, the symphony, museums, and other events were not foreign to us because our parents made concerted efforts to expose us to all things good, by their standards and by those of America.

"Nick" and Nettie not only read to us, but they were readers themselves. It seems that I was reading from the time I was born. In fact I have no memory of ever learning how to read but do clearly remember Mama reading to me from a very early age. By the time I entered first grade, my teacher, Mrs. I. Griffin, assigned me to the highest reading group (blue birds) stationed right by the entrance of our classroom at good ole' Bonner Elementary which was added to the National Registry of Historic Places in 1996. Many years later, her daughter gifted me with a set of the very same Alice and Jerry books from Mrs. Griffin's collection that I enjoyed in her first-grade class. Needless to say, I was honored and humbled by this priceless gift and most generous gesture.

Dad read the newspaper every single day cover to cover, and when or if provoked, heartily voiced his opinions regarding the issues of the day. He loved reading sports-related articles as well as material related to flowers and plants. He maintained a folder with articles and information collected on horticulture and the like and referenced them often.

He diligently worked to keep our property as eye-catching as he could; always outside in the yard especially weekends. There was always something to do; cutting, edging, planting, pruning or harvesting peppers, citrus, avocado, papaya and even an occasional pineapple whose sweetness rivaled those in Hawaii! Pops could grow just about anything beautifully. He loved showing you what he was growing and proudly discussed every aspect of yard and garden. The city of Daytona Beach honored my father's efforts with the Beautification Award which graced our yard for weeks.

Pops' backyard citrus trees were a sight to behold; their fragrant blossoms permeated the summer air, and shortly thereafter small oranges and grapefruit began to peek through for winter harvesting. I relish and appreciate the many years of fertilizing, pruning, and watering dedicated to making his fruit the best all around! It was such a thrill to take a few steps from our back door and top off breakfast with a ruby red or yellow grapefruit or orange fresh from our trees. We thought we were in heaven with all of this glorious fruit at our fingertips.

Pops also planted mango seeds on both the north and eastern side of our backyard. Those seeds were remnants from the fresh fruit devoured on our summer road trips to Fort Myers but planted many years after the citrus. I think he was experimenting with the southwest Florida tropical seed in central Florida ground. When we were little, no one else in Daytona even had a mango tree of which we were aware, so my dad tried his very skilled hand at planting those seeds in our fertile backyard far enough away from the citrus, so as not to interfere with their growth. The mango seeds were planted many years after the citrus. About eight months after his passing, the tree on the north side of our home bore a crop of sweet, juicy, stringy "pleasure;" mangoes had finally come to Daytona Beach, or at the least our own backyard. Hallelujah!

I guard his collection of articles and reference books closely. Needless to say, everything I know about gardening and lawn care, I learned expertly from my father.

Pops planted a garden of tomatoes, sugar cane, collard greens, pole beans, squash, and peppers in the backyard of my very first home. It was a sight to see; flourishing for a few years until I married in 1994. We ate and shared our bounty with many. Dad's garden was as much my pride and joy as was his. In fact I think the tomatoes in particular played a small role in my eventual marriage.

A few months after we started dating, my future husband "discovered," much to his surprise, that Pops had not only planted a generous garden but that patch of fruitful earth was rich with gorgeous tomatoes. I had no idea how much he loved tomatoes until he sauntered out to my backyard gold mine and returned to the house with tomatoes in hand and one in his mouth!

Having grown up in Fort Myers, Florida, it was no surprise that my parents and my mother in particular knew the names of practically every flower and plant there was. Fort Myers, AKA the city of palms, boasts a wonderland of flowers and plants, the envy of anywhere in the world. Whatever we grew here on the east coast grew seemingly twice as large and twice as abundantly there; bougainvillea, crape myrtle, lantana, roses, avocado, papaya, mango, hydrangea, and royal Poinciana. You name it. Mom could identify in an instant any plant, flower, or even weeds.

Mom was always taking cuttings from our yard to create small arrangements for any room or unexpected nook in our home. She was a master flower arranger, sharing her gift with many a person in hospital and home. I will never forget the many first days of school during my teaching career and other days when her creations graced my desk. I still have the first pair of book-ends, vase and encouraging note Mom gave me celebrating my very first teaching assignment in 1978. All of those thrift store vases and those saved when we received arrangements came in handy. Like Dad's collection of articles, I also inherited her vases and both their penchants for nature's greenery.

You don't have to convince me that nurturing and developing an appreciation for beauty in nature or elsewhere is one of the most meaningful and enduring gifts you can give to anyone.

An avid reader, too, I remember seeing Mom stretched out on the sofa in the living room enjoying both fiction and non-fiction, particularly the likes of James Baldwin, Theodore White, and John Grisham, the latter about whom she bragged having read all of his books. I think she read all of Baldwin's as well.

Our family library included two sets of encyclopedias, which we all used to help with assignments and supplement our research. My mother guarded those encyclopedias like a lioness protecting her cubs. She once accused my dad of taking one of the volumes "down the street" to help prove a point to one of his buddies. I don't recall whether we ever got it back.

Lastly Mom read to us regularly and enthusiastically. She read *The Night Before Christmas* with such conviction and animation that I believed in Santa until the age of sixteen! Just kidding. In all candor, if you want your kids to model good things, then you must engage in and expose them to good things as well. My parents' enjoyment of reading, as well as their appreciation for beauty and a love of learning, have made us richer and more whole people.

World War II Honoree

World War II Veteran

William Henry 'Nick' Ryan

BRANCH OF SERVICE
U.S. Army

HOMETOWN
Fort Myers, FL

HONORED BY
**Patricia Ryan-Ikegwuonu,
Esq., Daughter**

ACTIVITY DURING WWII

SERVED IN THE UNITED STATES ARMY, INDUCTED DECEMBER 5, 1942
AND ENLISTING INTO ACTIVE SERVICE DECEMBER 12, 1942 AT CAMP
BLANDING, FLORIDA. MEMBER OF THE 742ND ARTILLERY GUN BATTALION
SERVING IN THE PACIFIC THEATER. MILITARY OCCUPATIONAL SPECIALTY:
RADAR OPERATIONS ANALYST/TPQ 842. BATTLES AND CAMPAIGNS:
BISMARCK ARCHIPELAGO. DECORATIONS AND CITATIONS: WWII VICTORY
MEDAL, GOOD CONDUCT MEDAL, AND ASIATIC-PACIFIC THEATER MEDAL.
RECEIVED AN HONORABLE DISCHARGE JANUARY 3, 1946 AT CAMP
BLANDING, FLORIDA.

World War II Honoree

Nettie Cox Hawkins Ryan

BRANCH OF SERVICE
U.S. Army

HOMETOWN
Fort Myers, FL

HONORED BY
**Patricia Ryan-Ikegwuonu,
Esq., Daughter**

ACTIVITY DURING WWII

SERVED STATESIDE IN THE WOMEN'S ARMY CORPS (WAC), ENLISTING AUGUST 28, 1944, AND ENTERING ACTIVE SERVICE SEPTEMBER 6, 1944 IN TAMPA, FLORIDA. MILITARY OCCUPATIONAL SPECIALTY: CLERK GENERAL (055); ATTENDED DENTAL TECH SCHOOL AND GRADUATED FROM THE CLERK'S COURSE IN DES MOINES, IOWA IN JANUARY, 1945. DECORATIONS AND CITATIONS: WWII VICTORY MEDAL, GOOD CONDUCT MEDAL, AND AMERICAN THEATRE SERVICE MEDAL. HIGHEST GRADE HELD: T/5. RECEIVED AN HONORABLE DISCHARGE JULY 5, 1946 IN FORT BRAGG, NORTH CAROLINA.

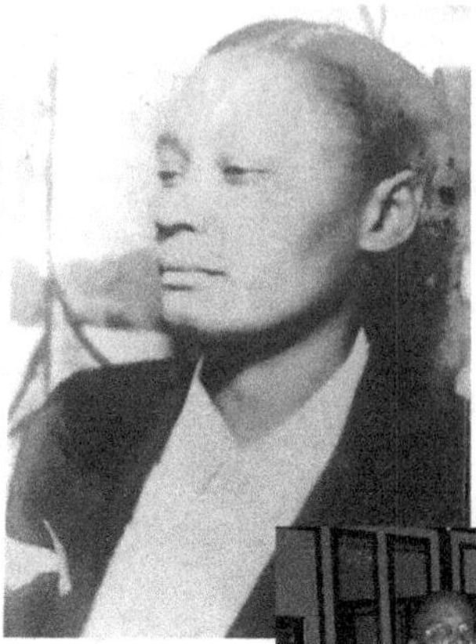

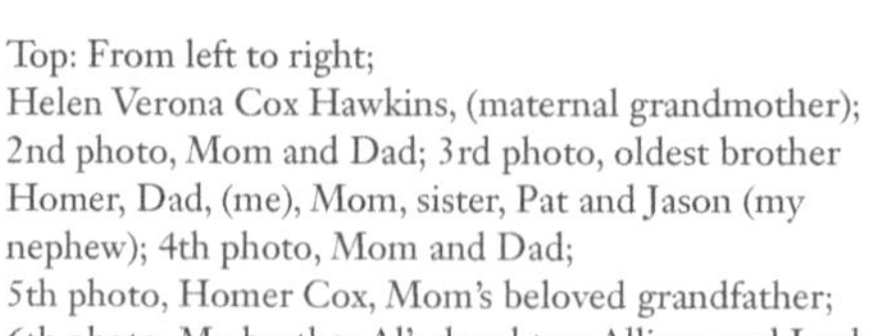

Top: From left to right;
Helen Verona Cox Hawkins, (maternal grandmother);
2nd photo, Mom and Dad; 3rd photo, oldest brother
Homer, Dad, (me), Mom, sister, Pat and Jason (my
nephew); 4th photo, Mom and Dad;
5th photo, Homer Cox, Mom's beloved grandfather;
6th photo, My brother Al's daughters Allison and Layla

Top: Dad (far left) with his buddies in the Pacific (WWII); LSO musicians Robert Turner and Hillary Jones performing in Mom's living room (Mom seated left); Laura's son Mason-Ryan in Arizona 2021; Mom and all her kids on her 90th birthday!

BEAUTIFICATION WINNERS

August Beautification Awards, presented by the City of Daytona Beach, went to the home of Mr. and Mrs William Ryan, 215 DeSoto St., above, and Volusia Plaza shopping center, 359 Jimmy Ann Drive.

Top: Dad behind the bar; 2nd photo, Mom with WAC, WWII; 3rd photo, our dad's award-winning yard!; 4th photo, My nephew Charles Karl and his wife Courtney

World War II Honoree

World War II Veteran

William Henry 'Nick' Ryan

BRANCH OF SERVICE
U.S. Army

HOMETOWN
Fort Myers, FL

HONORED BY
**Patricia Ryan-Ikegwuonu,
Esq., Daughter**

ACTIVITY DURING WWII

SERVED IN THE UNITED STATES ARMY, INDUCTED DECEMBER 5, 1942 AND ENLISTING INTO ACTIVE SERVICE DECEMBER 12, 1942 AT CAMP BLANDING, FLORIDA. MEMBER OF THE 742ND ARTILLERY GUN BATTALION SERVING IN THE PACIFIC THEATER. MILITARY OCCUPATIONAL SPECIALTY: RADAR OPERATIONS ANALYST/TPQ 842. BATTLES AND CAMPAIGNS: BISMARCK ARCHIPELAGO. DECORATIONS AND CITATIONS: WWII VICTORY MEDAL, GOOD CONDUCT MEDAL, AND ASIATIC-PACIFIC THEATER MEDAL. RECEIVED AN HONORABLE DISCHARGE JANUARY 3, 1946 AT CAMP BLANDING, FLORIDA.

Top: Dad's military service history; 2nd photo, Grandpa and Grandma Ryan; 3rd photo, President Obama recognizes Dad's service to country; 4th photo, Letter from Food Fair

The United States of America

honors the memory of

William H. Ryan, Jr.

This certificate is awarded by a grateful nation in recognition of devoted and selfless consecration to the service of our country in the Armed Forces of the United States.

President of the United States

FOOD FAIR STORES, INC.

2125 EAST ALLEGHENY AVENUE

PHILADELPHIA 34, PA.

MYER B MARCUS
EXECUTIVE VICE-PRESIDENT

Dear Mr. Ryan:

I am delighted to inform you that you have been nominated for an "E" Award in recognition of the effective job you are doing. Please accept my best wishes and congratulations.

You are now in competition with many of your co-workers who have received similar nominations. From among this group of outstanding men and women, our final "E" Award recipients will be selected when the program ends in April 1962.

I wish you good luck and all possible success in your efforts to win an "E"....and in your career with Food Fair.

Keep up the splendid work!

Sincerely,

Myer B. Marcus,
Executive Vice President

ml
October 25, 1961

Top: Mom and Dad, late teens/early 20's; 2nd photo, Niece Allison and daughters Arleigh and AuBrynne; 3rd photo, Mom (seated) on her 90th birthday May 15, 2015. From left nephew Charles, brother Charles, Alfred, Homer, close family friend, Marjorie G. Mitchell, (me), sister Laura, Pat, niece Allison on the end; front row, grand niece AuBrynne, Mom and nephew Mason-Ryan.

Top center photo; Dad at Daytona family reunion. Center left photo; My sister Pat &family friend Marjorie Gilmore Mitchell at Mom's 75th Birthday party. Center right photo; Dad at a wedding. Bottom left photo; Helen with former 'Miss America' Suzette Charles in Las Vegas 1990

Dad (far right) with Fort Myers friends; Center left; Mom and Dad at my brother Al's wedding in Chicago 1995. Center right; Mom's last visit to Daytona Beach VA Jan 2017. Bottom photo; Mom with her "girls" at 90th birthday party, sister in "love" Rebecca, my sister, Laura, family friend, Rhonda Robinson(Marjorie's daughter), my sister, Pat, me and Mom.

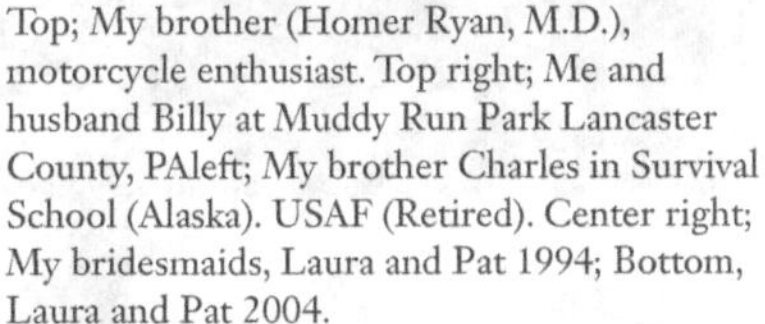

Top; My brother (Homer Ryan, M.D.), motorcycle enthusiast. Top right; Me and husband Billy at Muddy Run Park Lancaster County, PAleft; My brother Charles in Survival School (Alaska). USAF (Retired). Center right; My bridesmaids, Laura and Pat 1994; Bottom, Laura and Pat 2004.

Top photo my sister and brother, Attorneys Pat and Al, on the Daytona Beach pier; Center left; Nephew Charles, brother in law, Ike, nephew Jason and wife Kristina, nephew Mason and Pat. Third photo from top; Mom, Jason, and Laura. Bottom; Mom (on right) campaigning for YVONNE-SCARLETT GOLDEN (1st black mayor of Daytona Beach, FL).

Top ;Kristina Jason, Charles and their dad, Charles. Center left; Charles Karl on Tallahassee baseball team; Center right Laura's son Mason-Ryan ready for 8th grade dance. Bottom; "Lefty" Cox (Marcellus Douglas Cox) far right, middle row with Negro league farm team. "Lefty" was Mom's uncle.

Inscription at entrance of RYAN OBSERVATORY AT MUDDY RUN in Lancaster County PA; Center left; Al and I standing beside the inscription. Center right; yours truly on one side of the sign to the observatory designed by Al's wife Barbara. Bottom; Al standing at the Layla S Ryan Observatory in Glenside, PA.

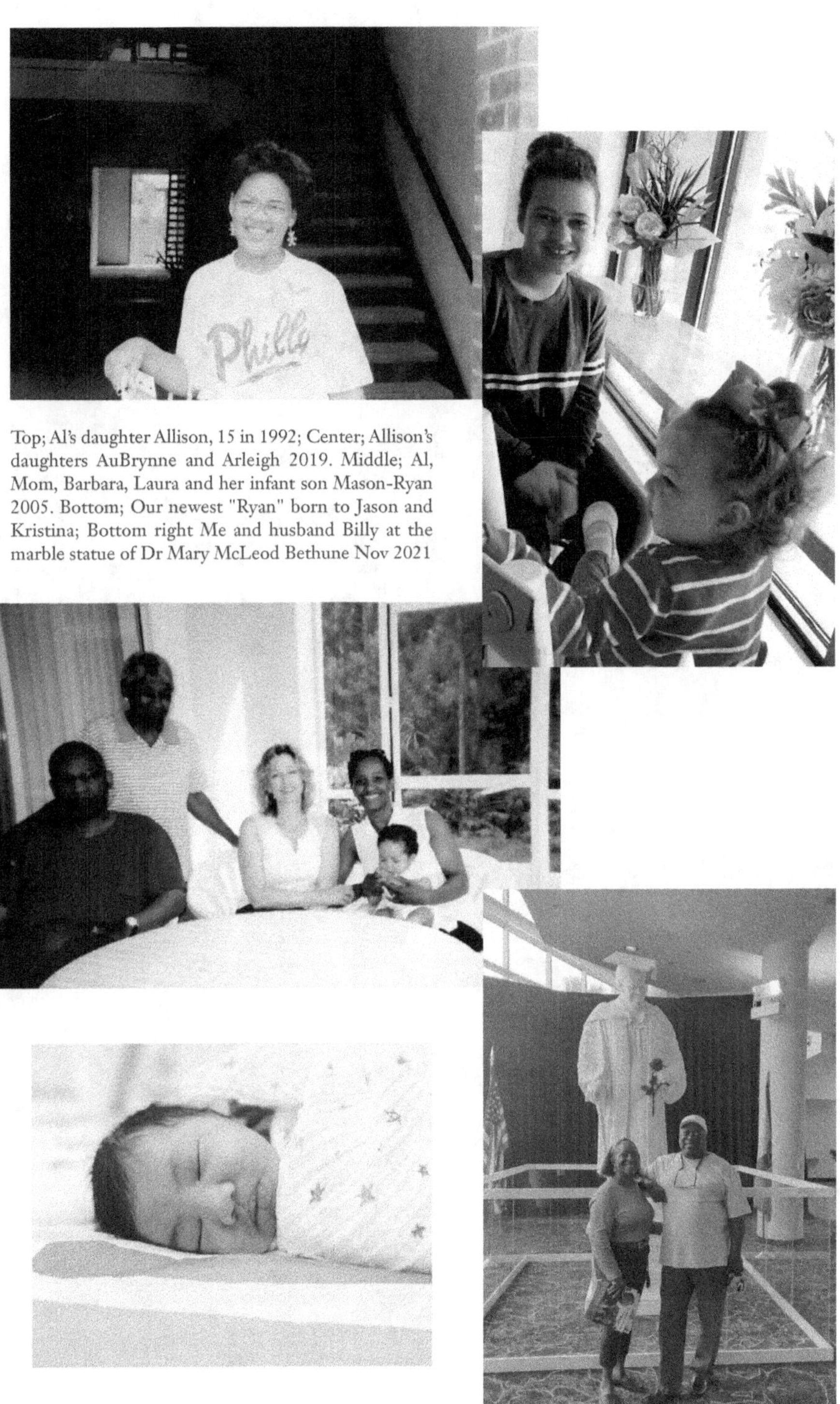

Top; Al's daughter Allison, 15 in 1992; Center; Allison's daughters AuBrynne and Arleigh 2019. Middle; Al, Mom, Barbara, Laura and her infant son Mason-Ryan 2005. Bottom; Our newest "Ryan" born to Jason and Kristina; Bottom right Me and husband Billy at the marble statue of Dr Mary McLeod Bethune Nov 2021

Get to Know Your Parents

A well-known author, Kahlil Gibran, said that "children learn what they live." So true. My mother used to say that children must be carefully taught. I learned later that she lifted that phrase from the Broadway musical, *South Pacific*, in which one of the characters said that children are not born hating others that they must be carefully taught to hate. Mom lifted the "carefully taught" part and turned it into a positive; that they must be carefully taught if you want lessons to "stick." Here's a freebie before we actually get into this book. Mom often quoted from literature and theatre to illustrate a lesson she was trying to teach us. My point being, that books, including the biblical book of Proverbs, as well as the arts contain a wealth of anecdotes and useful metaphors you may call upon to aid in your parenting "journey."

She didn't have a problem repeating herself a "million" times when she wanted to drive home a point or when she wanted you to modify your behavior. I don't know who coined the phrase, "practice makes perfect," but repetition was certainly a tried and true method utilized on a daily basis. If you weren't one of the six Ryan kids being admonished at any given moment, you certainly learned a lesson from your other siblings who were.

Dad said what he had to say only once; rarely did he repeat himself. We all knew that his temperament did not permit the kind of "back and forth" inquiries of parents from children so much more prevalent today. Whether or not you liked him or his admonitions was of no concern to him.

His parenting style differed sharply from Mom's. Children should be seen and not heard was one of his beliefs, coupled with, "Do as I say and not as I do." As for opinions, they were rarely welcomed, especially when he was in the process of disciplining or chastising us. Furthermore it was evident based upon demeanor that he had neither the patience, let alone the time to listen to a litany of explanations, excuses, or opinions from half a dozen "mouthy" dependents.

We later, armed with a little more wisdom and understanding, surmised that in some ways, the fact that Mom was an only child with extremely doting grandparents and Dad was raised in a family of six, including his rather stern parents, made all the difference in their approach to parenting. Mom spanked but preferred the "lecture circuit" replete with tried and true sayings and "mother wit." Dad's parents, we learned, had no problem using a switch or even their bare hands when they deemed necessary, and my dad executed punishment in the same manner. Dad was often baffled by our attempts to explain our misbehavior or lapses in judgement as he was big on using "common sense" as well as logic. To this day, I don't believe Dad ever understood our adolescent decision-making methodology.

He'd shake his head and say, "One day you gon learn," or, "Mark my word…." At any rate, with all of our collective failings as children and young adults, our parents managed to raise and ultimately produce six children netting two Bachelor's and one Master's Degree, two Juris Doctors (Doctors of Law) and one Medical Doctor (M.D.).

Dad's family worked hard for everything they had. At one time, my paternal grandparents, Henry and Onie (not Annie) Ryan, owned and operated a beer parlor in the black section of Fort Myers, Florida. Their business was located in the heart of black Fort Myers on Anderson Avenue, re-named Dr. Martin Luther King Jr. Blvd. Uncle Julius, his older brother by five years, had to quit school before finishing sixth grade to work and help the family make ends meet. And though Dad was spoiled (we always heard he was his mother's favorite), he and his two brothers, the other named Charles and one sister Lillian, always had chores.

I don't know how my grandmother even occasionally helped Grandpa at the beer parlor and maintain a home so clean, "You could eat off the floor" as my mother would say. My grandparents' hard wood floors were always immaculate, furniture polished as shiny diamonds, and everything had a place; no extraneous anything, which was a source of angst where Mom was concerned. It was as if home keeping (long before Martha Stewart coined the phrase) were a science to be mastered, but not in Mom's book. You could just say that it was not on the top of her "must do" list. Grandma, on the other hand, was obsessive about having a clean house.

Mom's memories of Grandma sort of hurrying us from the breakfast table to help clean up never left her. It's funny, though Dad grew up with a mom who was passionate about cleanliness, he was not a slave-driver about cleaning; he left Mom in charge of that and was, for the most part, comfortable about the way our home was maintained.

He often spoke of the modest gifts they received at Christmas, or any occasion; a shoebox filled mostly with fruit (especially citrus), nuts, and hard candy. During the holidays, Pops always purchased a canister of those multi-colored hard candies reminiscent of his childhood Christmases. He lounged in his easy chair savoring the sweet confections marking that special time of year.

Holidays or not, Dad was a serious chocolate lover. You might open our refrigerator at any moment and put your hands on a Hershey or Snickers candy bar. It seems the older he got, the more he consumed. Not so surprising that a giant Hershey bar was a sure-fire way to make his Christmas a mite merrier!

If you really want to understand what makes your parents "tick," try to ascertain as well as understand as much about their family dynamics as possible. What was their birth order? Were they only children? Were they raised by a single parent or one who may have been emotionally "absent?" Were there strong influences from other relatives? Did their parents live to see them grow up? If not, who stepped into that parenting or guardianship role if one or both parents were no longer present? In what part of the country were they raised, and what values most influenced their families? Of course a host of other factors could very well have played a role in the way our parents chose to raise us. My advice: Get to know your parents. Ask questions. Talk to them. I certainly wished that I had done so more often.

Thank you for the privilege of sharing with parents, would be-parents, grandparents, guardians, caring adults, and caregivers a little more of the "father wit" and "mother wit" that has served us well from two of the greatest role-models any child could ever have.

REMEMBER, YOU'VE GOT SISTERS!

A few years after Mom retired from the classroom, she opened a child care business in her home. About five years prior to the opening, Mom worked with state and city inspectors to modify her home according to code in order to accommodate her prospective charges. Initially she was excited about caring for young babies (her first choice), but shortly thereafter, Mom realized that at her age infants were a bit of a "stretch."

She soon discovered that caring for three and four-year-old preschoolers more fulfilling than she could ever imagine. I have fond memories of the brightest and most beautiful and delightful boys and girls imaginable. They ranged from shy and demure to energetic, rambunctious, thoughtful, and engaging. Needless to say, their parents and grandparents were already doing a tremendous job with them, and as they matured, it became more and more apparent that their consistent and attentive parenting skills rewarded them adults who would make anyone proud. Several of the girls continued to foster their relationship with Mom until her passing.

By the time Mom opened her child care business, our parents had raised six children, all of whom graduating from college and beyond.

She always stressed to her little charges that "respect and honor to all is due," regardless of one's station in life. And as it pertained to my three older brothers, women in particular. She quickly addressed any disrespectful or negative comments with respect to women. My younger sisters and I were always curious when Mom addressed issues pertaining to their female friends or girlfriends.

Mom firmly believed that we reap what we sow, and by encouraging the boys to behave respectfully towards women and girls, she was opening the door for her own daughters to reap healthy relationships with others. I think Mom was trying to attract the best for her girls by teaching her sons to behave respectfully.

Whenever she detected even a hint of irreverence directed towards women, she very promptly declared, "Remember you've got sisters!"

The old adage about the way in which you treat your mom as a barometer for the way you will treat your wife ties in nicely with the lesson illustrated here. After all your mom was once a girl, too.

Always Ask to Speak to the Wife First

Telephone etiquette like the dinosaur seems to have become extinct. Is it possible that the ubiquity of the internet/social media and texting has rendered the proper use of the telephone, passé? Social media and cell phones were non-existent during my formative years and well into adulthood; the stationary telephone was the order of the day. Among the myriad of lessons we were taught, using the telephone properly was certainly one of them. When placing a call, we had to identify ourselves first, then state the reason for our call.

There was one area of telephone etiquette that Mom was particularly sensitive about, and those were the rare occasions when we telephoned the residence of a married couple. If I or one of my sisters phoned such residences and needed to speak with the "Mr." for example, and who may have in fact answered the phone, we were taught to greet the "Mr." politely but ask to speak with his wife first. After greeting her, we then stated our purpose for calling, and she would either relay our message or concerns to him or hand the phone to her husband.

We were most likely making a business call for our parents. Many of the craftsman, skilled laborers, tailors, etc. or other business owners with whom we dealt were people our family had known for years. Also, in the sixties, seventies, and early eighties, most were African-American and deeply rooted in our community. This measure of courtesy became more important particularly as we matured and was for the most part emphasized to us girls more than our brothers. But the reverse would have applied equally to them in similar situations.

Why the seemingly unnecessary effort illustrated in the above example? Firstly, we acknowledge the lady of the house out of respect. Secondly, she feels more confident that your intentions are honest and above-board, and thirdly, she doesn't have to ask her husband the question that shouldn't be annoying but indeed can be: "Honey, who was that calling?"

Trust me, the "Mrs." is secretly appreciative that you afforded her the courtesy of identifying yourself, and it shows your regard for their marriage or relationship. Of course relationships differ in a myriad of ways, and my example may not "fit" any of your interactions with people, but you may be surprised at the way in which this extra measure of courtesy goes a very long way.

LOOK AT PEOPLE: ADDRESS THEM OR CALL THEM BY NAME

As my parents aged, it became clearer to me why it is critically important to address people or call them by name when you want their attention. Aging puts more demands on the senses, especially the auditory and visual. It is vital that those whose senses are in fact compromised be given the opportunity whenever possible to hear us the first time. The loss of precious seconds so crucial in emergencies, for example, could be prevented if we seek first to get other's attention rather than to assume they hear us. If you are already engaged in conversation, it isn't necessary to continue to call the other person's name, however if you and your intended receiver are engaged in separate activities in the same general vicinity, you wouldn't begin to converse without first getting their attention. Often people hear but don't understand. Some who suffer hearing loss have learned to read lips, but that works only if they're looking at you.

For some reason, people seem to equate diminished auditory acuity with the loss of mental acumen more than the loss of visual acuity. People who constantly ask that something be repeated are often viewed with resentment, disdain, or at minimum, impatience. On the contrary, compromised vision obviously doesn't prompt one to utter such questions as, "What did you say?", "Would you repeat that please?" But it may require audible interpretation or some form of physical assistance.

Sometimes the sender of the message shows an impatience, which may cause the intended recipient of the message to "shut down," become more reclusive, or even worse, "pretend" to hear you, which may prove hazardous. And if you are not in the same room with the person with whom you're communicating, that is a sure-fire recipe for trouble. It's like trying to cook "out of the kitchen." Does not work.

Let's take a moment to turn toward people and look them in the eye before addressing them, especially the elderly, and in many cases, children too. This shows consideration and increases the likelihood of more effective communication.

This lesson was really brought home to me as my mother aged. Her hearing, like Dad's, became progressively worse.

In my frustration triggered when I thoughtlessly began a conversation without getting her attention, she finally said, in her equally frustrated tone, "Helen, you have to say 'Mama' first; get my attention, then I'll respond." Dad, on the other hand, had a history of conditions related to his hearing and visited an ear, nose, and throat doctor for those maladies. In ensuing years, he was prescribed hearing aids but refused to wear them.

In summary we have to intentionally implement practices to more effectively and enjoyably communicate with those whose senses may be compromised.

Go To the Bathroom
as soon as You Awaken

We spent most of our childhood in the home our parents built in 1960. It was a modest mid-century modern flat roof house with three bedrooms, kitchen, living and dining areas, one bathroom, and a one-car carport later converted into a "Florida" room. In the mid-seventies, an addition was built onto the back of our house, which included a second bath and even more living space!

We moved into our 215 Desoto Street home in February 1961. At that time, there were about twelve established families living there; a quarter of them headed by both mother and father, another by a single/divorced/widowed mother, and the remainder were grandparents or aunts and uncles raising their grandchildren or nephews and nieces. We were among the first group and quickly became acquainted with every family on our street.

Much of our growing fellowship with our neighbors was due in part to my mother's friendly and welcoming demeanor and her firm belief that good neighbors were essential and contributory to the development of successful, productive, and harmonious community. This philosophy was nurtured in part by the way in which she was reared and most probably further solidified by her decision to major in the social sciences in college.

Mornings were especially challenging when seven people (eight by the time my youngest sister was born in 1964) had to prepare for work and school; when we moved there, I was five-years-old, but it wasn't until my twentieth birthday that we added a second bathroom. By then my three older brothers had long gone, however we all had to learn many years earlier how to manage with the one bathroom.

For starters, in order to save time in the mornings, we were encouraged to prepare our clothes the night before, including accessories, such as shoes, socks, undergarments. Whether we were bussed to school, being driven, or hiking, it just made since to prepare ahead rather than scramble for apparel in the mornings. Sometimes we missed the mark and indeed rush to figure out just what to wear. Secondly, during the winter months, we were encouraged to bathe the night before and do a time-saving quick wash-up next morning.

Most importantly though, we were urged to go to the bathroom as soon as we awakened. One could avoid a serious "accident" by getting in the bathroom immediately. If you had to go back in to wash up, at least you didn't have to resort to dancing a "jig" in the interim.

We didn't all have the same schedule, so we'd run to the kitchen for breakfast, then return to our room to dress for school or return to the bathroom if need be.

Mom had the foresight to have saved a potty chair from mine and my middle sister's training days. It came in handy when we as very young girls absolutely could not wait to get into the bathroom. We learned to use, empty, rinse, and add a little bleach to the removable potty part and then return it to a designated corner in the bathroom hallway. We kept that chair until my youngest sister was trained; of course by the time she was six, all of my brothers were off to college or professional school, so she never had to "jockey" for her place in the bathroom!

Wait for an Invitation

A "pet peeve" of my mother's was to never attend an invitation only event when you have not received an invitation yourself. She was extremely passionate about this almost to a fault. If one is working within the framework of a budget, this factor alone determines the number of guests, the amount of food, drinks, decorations, seating, entertainment, and the cost of purchasing and mailing invitations. So if you are the hostess and someone decides to attend your affair without having received an invitation, they have in effect "crashed" your party by upsetting the dynamics of your plans.

Regardless of the size and scope of the affair, many functions are highly personal and often theme specific. For example, a party for a wounded veteran returning from combat, a ninetieth birthday celebration, college classmates and their families, fishing aficionados, wine and cheese lovers, a prayer group, or a few "select" guests with certain things in common might mean that you don't receive an invitation, even if you happen to know some of the guests!

When my mother hosted members of the London Symphony Orchestra in her home a number of years ago, she thought long and hard about her guest list. Considering the size of her home as well as the musicians, their instruments, and the space they needed, Mom was extremely careful about the number of guests she felt she could most comfortably accommodate. She could not focus on the scores of people she certainly would like to have invited, nor what would they say not having been invited. Instead her focus had to be on accommodating her orchestra guests above all else.

We need to allow others the prerogative of hosting an event and inviting whomever they wish without being questioned. I have witnessed such lapses in manners when others dared "force" my mother into such an awkward position.

If a friend invites you to accompany him or her to an invitation only affair and you have not received an invitation, I would strongly advise that you consider not attending for reasons stated at the top of this essay. A very good friend of mine prevailed upon me to attend a special event with her for one of her relatives a few years ago. She assured me that it was perfectly alright for me to attend. Although it was tempting and I almost gave in to her pleas (as I discerned a reluctance on her part about attending alone), I could not for the life of me (or my friend) accompany her.

My mother's voice kept nagging at me, "Wait for an invitation," with all the emphasis on the word "wait." Yes, my friend had indeed invited me, but since I had not received a formal invite, I simply could not attend.

I am not advising this nor would my mother, however the best you can do if you wish to invite someone to accompany you to an affair for which they have not received an invitation would be to phone the host and ask permission to bring your friend. Most of the time they'll say yes when they really want to say no. It's not fair to put them in that position though. I'll tell you what, plan a party for thirty and have six of your guests bring one additional person. Six more people means more food, beverages, seating, and even adjusting your air conditioning. Best to wait for an invitation.

Wait to Be Invited

Mama was equally opposed to the idea of uninvited houseguests, though most who lodged with us were either invited or expected; I do not recall having to accommodate anyone in our home who didn't fit into one of those categories, but believe me when I tell you that we heard more than a few "horror" stories from others not afforded such courtesies. Irrespective of how close you are or how close you may think you are to someone, it really is good manners to ask in advance to stay with others in their home rather than to assume that you are welcome at any time.

Your potential hostess may be swamped with work, in the middle of a project, expecting company, "under the weather," or simply prefer not having guests at the time that you wish to stay. And what is most often the case, your host may feel uncomfortable telling you no as she employs every bit of diplomacy to reduce the possibility of hurt feelings or disappointment. Hosting "uninvited guests" is like trying to host a party with insufficient funds; even if you are a party of one, it's a scramble trying to make things run smoothly.

Do not put anyone, even close friends, in this position; call first and allow them the liberty of saying yes or no. If your friends or family have spouses and/or children, they may need to juggle schedules or other obligations in order to accommodate you. Show consideration for others, no matter their relationship.

There are, on the other hand, exceptions to almost any rule; you may find on your life's journey at least one or two people whose doors are always open to you, and most of us know right off the bat who those individuals are.

Let's assume your potential host has uttered those most welcoming of words. "Of course you may stay. Wouldn't have it any other way." What are your responsibilities once there? Here are a few you may wish to ponder with the "golden rule" as your guiding principle. Make yourself at home, but respect others' home as you would wish them to respect yours. 1) If they receive a phone call, make yourself scarce. 2) Tidy up behind yourself. 3) Offer to prepare a meal or invite them out. 4) Do not make unreasonable requests e.g. asking for steak when fish is on the dinner menu would be a breach of good manners. If you are allergic to certain foods, politely make that known to your host. 5) Make every effort to maintain an atmosphere of good will in your conversation and by your behavior. 6) Find time to amuse yourself; even welcoming hostesses need a little "break." Take a nap, go for a walk, sit outside and read, listen to music, or play games. Visit a special site or go for a ride around town. 7) Leave things better than when you found them.

Some people are gifted with the spirit of hospitality, and when on the receiving end, this is most fulfilling for both you and your host. There is nothing more gratifying than sharing the beauty of a friend's garden, the adventure of a long-awaited fishing trip, a slice of delicious homemade cake or pie, a beautiful craft, or photos from times gone by. Just being in their presence is like being in a warm and cozy place most probably akin to your own home.

In order to maintain good feelings at all times, call or in some way contact a potential host and let them know you'd like to be a guest in their home for a few days or overnight if that's the case. As previously stated, there are probably one or two people in your life whose homes are always open to you, but they're the exception. It's best to contact your potential hosts first, or better yet, wait to be invited.

WEAR SENSIBLE SHOES

Some of the most contentious arguments between Mom, me, and my sister prior to leaving for school were about our attire. Mama had very definite standards as it pertained to dress, and those standards often clashed with what we deemed "in or out of style." Just because it was fashionable didn't mean that it was appropriate for us or for the occasion. This was especially true when it came to our choice of shoes. If Mom had her way, we'd be in saddle oxfords or Mary Janes with socks every day!

Well, that just wasn't going to cut it considering the wild styles of the late sixties and early seventies when my sister Pat and I were approaching our teens. I was pretty much compliant when it came to wearing what I was told and leaned more toward the conservative anyway, but Pat was definitely more in tune to styles and trends and more inclined to want to wear what she preferred. Their differing viewpoints produced a few "lively" exchanges before heading out the door.

Rain boots, for example, were certainly not an everyday shoe that Mom would have made us wear, but it fits in the category of both sensible and sometimes necessary. What sensible shoes looked like where Mom was concerned will be defined in a few moments, and of course the sometimes necessary rain boots were worn over those sensible shoes. Mom wore hers as we grew up, but I didn't get "smart" until later. Seems one of us owned a pair of those yellow boots, but somehow as we matured, she chose not to fight this particular battle with us. She knew we'd rather do anything except show up in school in a pair of rubber rain boots, no matter how wet our shoes became or how soggy our socks or hose.

The ones I wore as a social worker were actually ones "inherited" from Mom. My travels from office to schools, homes, agencies, and meetings all over the county in oftentimes drenching rains were a source of friendly teasing by co-workers but a welcomed motherly prescription for a downpour. I bought my own pair of the now stylish knee-length firefighter boots a decade or two later when my feet needed protection from water, weeds, dirt, and tall grass while working outdoors. Now the shoes toward which we once turned up our noses have been "resurrected" and displayed side by side other shoes in elite as well as discount stores.

Wearing what Mom believed to be "sensible" shoes on the one hand kept us looking like little girls a little longer. We also reduced our risk of falling, tripping, or slipping down by wearing shoes which were sturdy, slightly arched, often string-up as opposed to step-ins, and with a lower heel as opposed to those providing less support for our feet. Mom loved shoes and owned many in a variety of styles, almost always enhancing her gorgeous legs. But they were always fit for the occasion and always rendered her a measure of safety.

Let me share a little anecdote straight from the wisdom of a ten-year-old boy. Two kids, a boy, age ten, and a little girl, age eight, were racing towards the museum from my car. As they approached the building, the ten-year-old gently shoved the eight-year-old to help secure his victory to the door of course. The eight-year-old fell down and scraped her elbow and knee as a result of that "strategic" shove. Fortunately I was able to console the eight-year-old and render first aide inside the museum.

Upon returning home and sharing what happened, the ten-year-old reasoned, "Well, she had on the wrong shoes. It's okay to be fashionable but sometimes fashionable can get ugly." You see she had on a pair of "jellies" with a sling back heel. Jellies, while perfect for the beach, are a little unstable for daily wear and most certainly will not help you win a sprint to anywhere. That precocious ten-year-old, now seventeen, is my nephew and his equally precocious cousin, (my great niece) then eight, is now fifteen.

Even then my nephew, wise beyond his years, recognized the folly and the danger of wearing the wrong shoes. Of course shoving his cousin didn't help matters either.

Use Your Good English/
Keep Your Voice Down

Both our parents were blessed with voices that "carried," especially when they had to. Pop's voice was fairly modulated; in fact you could almost describe him as soft-spoken on most days. But when he needed to make a point about something, his stern and decisive voice came through loudly and clearly.

If a discussion became particularly heated, he would interject with the query, "Am I right or wrong about it?" and of course he was always right about it! Those exchanges were usually reserved for his cronies or contemporaries; we were rarely afforded the privilege as children or adolescents of actually telling our dad that he was right or wrong about anything.

Mom was not soft-spoken, but she was clear and very positive when she opened her mouth. It was somewhat of an effort for her to modulate her tone; she always said that she didn't have a "sweet" voice, for which we totally disagreed. We loved her voice! She also said that we had "big" mouths, meaning loud like hers, and constantly admonished us to keep our tone well-modulated.

Mom was often misunderstood (she thought) because of the way in which she "came across" to people. She was definitely not a shrinking violet, and 99 percent of the time, meant no harm. She always wanted to be understood without any hint of ambiguity and certainly without sounding threatening or rude. She took pains to explain what she was trying to convey, especially as it pertained to what she thought was best for us. I wish that I had been less combative and quite honestly more respectful when Mom, at the point of exasperation or exhaustion declared, "I wouldn't lead you wrong."

During our formative years, conversations among me and my sisters often became a little loud or a little too heated to suit Mom. Often we were not even aware that the tone of our voices had risen considerably.

Mom, always monitoring and always listening, called out, "Girls, keep your voices down. You can be heard all the way to New Smyrna" (or Holly Hill, Deland). Again she was "old-school" and believed that young ladies should maintain well-modulated voices. Of course we thought this a bit extreme; after all we were in our own rooms just having fun. Nevertheless, just as sure as our voices dropped a few octaves, they gradually returned to the elevated level that got us in trouble in the first place. This time no admonitions but a swift and sure warning of separation, which meant we couldn't talk to one another, and that was pure "torture!"

Another thing that Mom always stressed was using as she described our "good English" at all times. Not only because it was proper, but in so doing, it might inspire others to look favorably upon us where opportunities were concerned. My parents grew up during a time when negative stereotypes about black people were pervasive in American society and allowed to flourish in a racial climate, which nourished such negativity amongst the white majority. Mama did everything she could to encourage our use of Standard English and proceeded to correct us as often as she saw fit. It was a little annoying on occasion, especially since correction was not reserved for us in private but also in the presence of anyone else. Incidentally there are more than a few of our neighborhood contemporaries who could testify to having been corrected by Mom as well.

My siblings would agree that the ability to express ourselves both with a level of fluency and grammatical acuity has helped open many doors in our journey through this life. Having served thirty-four years in education in at least six or seven different positions, I am certain that part of my success in "navigating" the larger society was in my ability to express myself with a degree of exceptionality.

Mom was a master of both oral and written expression; she was invited to speak on many occasions, usually on behalf of someone else and often extemporaneously. Her gift coupled with a winning smile and personality has been the perfect model to this day. She was often drafted to assist with a number of writing projects in the city and on behalf of individuals.

Summarily, teach children to modulate their voices in consideration of where they are and to use their very best grammar when expressing themselves. It really does make a difference.

Live Within Your Means

My dad's childhood was marked by having lived during the Great Depression. Born in the early 1920's and coming of age in the late thirties helped to shape his opinions about money and finances. He grew up in a family of six; at one time, his father was a small business owner having operated a beer parlor in Fort Myers, Florida. His mother was a homemaker and a darn good one. She kept their frame home immaculate and prepared the most delicious meals you have ever eaten.   In fact one of my earliest memories is having dropped a precious egg from the chicken coop on Grandma's polished hardwoods. Oops! And almost everyone had Hadin, turpentine, apple, and other varieties of mango trees on their property. We never failed to leave there without a bounty of mangoes destined to "fragrance" the four-hour drive home.

Mama was an only child raised primarily by her doting grandparents. Her mother was a teacher/principal at a little school in a town called Moore Haven, Florida. Grandma Helen commuted by bus from Fort Myers to Moore Haven every Sunday afternoon to prepare for work on Monday. She rode back home to Fort Myers on Friday afternoon for the weekend. She and Grandpa Elijah were divorced, but he worked as an assistant at a local pharmacy in Fort Myers. There was no point in my grandmother attempting to parent my mother on her weekend visits home because Grandma's parents (my great-grandparents) had become somewhat proprietary when it came to my mother; they felt entitled to chastise Mom or not since they were primarily responsible for her care. She was essentially spoiled, especially by her Grandpa Homer, who adored my mother as much as she adored him.

It helps to know something of your parent's background in order to understand their particular philosophy about money. Mom was free-hearted and generous, and Pops was not. Pops often spoke about the modest gifts they received at Christmas; a shoebox filled with hard candy, nuts, and fruit, and Mom spoke proudly (let's just say bragged) about growing up in a two-story house complete with a toilet upstairs and downstairs—something few black people had in the late twenties and early thirties when Mom was a girl. Her grandfather catered to her, and although we always heard that my paternal grandmother spoiled my father, he and his two brothers and one sister pulled together and worked to maintain their family business and held other jobs as well. Everybody pulled their load around the Ryan house, but my maternal grandparents didn't really require Mom to do very much, except attend school and church; that's it.

Pops really liked "nice" things and could just about sniff out what appeared to be the most expensive of items a mile away. I heard him once say that he was not trying to keep up with the Jones'; instead he was trying to surpass them! Practically everything Pops owned was well-made, and although you could describe him as frugal, even stingy at times, he could "smell" quality a mile away. He didn't drive expensive vehicles but never begrudged anyone else who did. I believe that automobiles were the one item he was very careful about purchasing because he had a family to care for and believed his money had to "stretch" in order to meet all of our needs.

Now clothing was quite another matter; we knew he took pride in his apparel and made wise, and in that sense, quality purchases. Although he appreciated what we gave him, we would always angst over our choices for him because of his penchant for the "best." He hardly ever spent "all" of his money on anything; there was always something left for a rainy day. He once responded most adamantly to me that he would never be "dead broke," and he wasn't. Pops and I had more than a few "go-arounds" about, get this, how he spent HIS money!

Mom encouraged an appreciation for all that we had. She discouraged any attempt on our part to feel we were lesser if we didn't have what others had. We were not competing with others and were not jealous either. We were absolutely not getting anything solely because someone else had it; if we happened to get it, fine but not because of anyone else. Mom believed in caring for what we had by keeping it clean and in good condition. There were six of us so when birthdays rolled around, the honoree was the only one receiving gifts and not the other siblings based upon the assumption that our feelings might be hurt. It was the honoree's special day, and when it was our turn, the same practice applied.

Sometimes shoes were purchased for either the boys or the girls, and when it was the other's turn, we received new shoes as well. We learned to celebrate each other's gifts and achievements rather than focus on what we did not have or were not receiving at the time.

It was not important to our parents that we have the latest or newest outfits or toys. We had what they could afford to give us, and sometimes it was indeed the newest or the latest. It was very important that we learn to appreciate all we did have. Just like many children in our sphere, we had our share of disappointments concerning a lot of things, but gratefulness was a virtue that Mom especially modeled and demanded. And by the way, she did not tolerate bullying nor were we allowed to pick on other people. Period. She couldn't stand name-calling, and neither did she like using nicknames believing some to convey negative and uncomplimentary messages, which might possibly have a negative effect on children for life. Mom believed people should be called by their name.

Manners and a Few Social Graces

We were taught manners and social graces primarily by our mom and mostly by imitating what she did, what she said, or the way in which she would re-act or not in any given situation. Mom had no problem correcting us in public, including our grammar (something few parents do these days). With regard to behavior, My mother always said that she was "raising us for the world and not just for her and my father," and because of this, she felt that it was incumbent upon her to teach us as much as possible just in case, for example, we might one day influence political and social policy, research cures for disease, teach children from diverse backgrounds, assist the homeless in our respective communities, encourage others to find themselves, lead platoons in the military, or a work crew for the city. No matter what we were likely to become or where in the world we would live, she wanted people to be glad to see us coming and hate to see us leave.

There is absolutely no way to chronicle all of the practical wisdom we were taught during the course of our developmental years, and by the way, our parents felt they had a "right" to continue teaching until their dying day by critiquing the manner in which we conducted ourselves, our business, or the way we interacted with others to some degree. Not as often as when we were kids, but they seemed to be on the look-out for behavior incongruent with what we were taught.

Allow me to comment on just a few of those little efforts to refine our behavior during our formative years:

Never say to your host (unless necessary) that you don't like something or that you don't eat certain foods. You may have an allergy to specific food items, which may make you sick (even if that particular food item touches other foods), or you may need to inform caregivers of the allergies of loved ones, that's different. But just to declare that you don't like or you don't eat certain foods is rude. Again, within the context of a conversation, it's permissible; otherwise leave it on your plate, or if offered, state ever so politely, "I don't care for any, thank you."

When the server comes around with hors d'oeuvres, take one, yes, only one at a time. The same applies to a tray of cookies- one cookie at a time please. Focus on the person with whom you are conversing and not the amount of food you can pile on a small plate or in the palm of your hands.

Eat before you leave home. Some people eat little or nothing during the day in order to save "room" for lots of food later. You need nourishment all during the day. Never depend on anyone else to feed you. The unexpected may occur, and you just may not have the occasion to eat at all.

Please, for the love of heaven, do not ask to take food home from a party or gathering. This is not good manners. Notice I said do not ask. If your host offers food, that's different, but again, be sensible; she is offering you the food, not anyone else.

Don't slide in your shoes. Pick up your feet and walk. Mom absolutely detested seeing women slide in their shoes. It just wasn't lady-like. I don't remember any reference to men or boys committing such an egregious error. Wipe or stomp your feet thoroughly before entering someone's home.

Look but don't touch. My siblings and I heard this every time we went out in public, especially shopping. Hold young children's hands and keep them very near you; do not allow running around any place of business. My parents were often complimented on how well-behaved we were, and we were often invited back to others' homes because of it. I remember quite vividly a visit by my nieces to visit their grandparents in Florida. They were preparing to go "window shopping" with Mom, but that concept was apparently foreign to them as they queried, "Window shopping, what's that?" Mom explained that it meant they weren't buying anything, just looking, and that they were to do just that. Mom did not want to be responsible for replacing items broken or damaged due to disobedience, carelessness, or unruly behavior.

I witnessed an incident recently involving a female parent, guardian, or relative, which was disturbing; two children around the age of three were running full throttle through a department store. Their mother was strolling through the store with one or two other women. She proceeded to use foul language as she called for the children to stop running. My sister and her son also observed this most egregious lapse in parental control.

First of all, they were much too young to be away from their parents, who obviously were too irresponsible to hold their hands. Secondly, the adults set a poor example for their young charges by employing unbecoming language with children who were too young to control themselves and therefore not responsible for their own behavior.

Rather than a simple "yes or no," it is better on occasion to respond with, "yes, I am/will or no, I am not," "no, I didn't," or "yes/no sir/ma'am."

Do not eat or drink in someone's vehicle without permission.

Do not touch or pick up mail or personal items in someone's home, office, etc.

Acknowledge gifts or thoughtful gestures with a note of thanks or phone call. No texts or emails please. Since Christmas is the season for giving, I would not think it necessary to acknowledge those gifts, however, if you wish to do so, it is always appropriate to say thank you and it is never too late either. And by the way, please name the gift or gesture specifically in your note of thanks. For example, "I will use the twenty dollars wisely. Thank you," is much better than a simple, "Thank you for the money."

Children should not be allowed to interfere, interrupt, or in any way indulge in conversations pertinent to adults. Parents must monitor appropriately. Mom used to say, "Stay in a child's place," or we had to leave the room.

Do not allow your children to run through the toy department of a business and proceed to play with the toys! I have seen children attempt to open packaging. Where are their parents?

Monitor what they say. They need to be told what is right and proper and that they are responsible for their words and actions. Correct their grammar and make them repeat it correctly and immediately. "Whatever," or "Yeah," "Okay" is unacceptable.

In conversation teach them to focus on others more than themselves. They should not brag about what they have or what they're going to get. Modesty is the best policy.

Teach or model concern for others. Mom did this all of our lives. She modeled compassion by sharing, encouraging, and extending herself with little niceties that helped make life richer for our family as well as for others.

Tidy up behind yourself or leave things better than when you found them. If you dropped it, pick it up, hang it up, or dispose of it properly. Don't wait for your mother, the maid, your teacher, the street sweeper, or the janitor to do it for you.

Tidy up or clean up around your front door as soon as you can in the morning. This is where you live whether you own or rent. Your front door is a reflection of you.

When you visit those having experienced a tragic or life-changing event, don't go empty-handed. Take the time to write a note or bring a card, flowers, food, or something; put some thought into what you're going to bring. Your recipients will always remember it.

Perhaps the Most Consequential of Lessons

The previous lessons, some practical and some more philosophical, were indeed meaningful to my parents, however, the one area in which Mom expressed the greatest regret was in the area of our spiritual growth and development; she truly regretted that we did not attend Sunday School and worship services more regularly than we did. I heard her express those sentiments on a number of occasions as my middle adult years took root and the sun "set" on Mom's. Based upon her experiences, as well as all she endured, she concluded that a strong spiritual foundation was most significant in helping to cope with all life brought her way.

My siblings and I attended Sunday school, but we usually walked those eight short blocks without our parents. Mom attended with us when she could, but in her defense, preparing breakfast for a family of six children and subsequently getting them ready for services was challenging, especially when you're married to a man of their generation (some of whom thought it Mom's "job" or duty to take care of certain tasks almost exclusively). Mom did not always have time to "prep" our Sunday dinner on Saturday, so rushing home from church to cook was a challenge to work through, among other things. Often my father was not as patient or understanding as he should have been, which made her "job" even more of an effort.

Though a source of concern at the time, the more "inebriated" citizens who settled along our route to Sunday School never really bothered us, and in hindsight, this was a comparatively "small thing," as Mama used to say, when you consider the more perverse and abominable activities children are currently exposed to both on the streets and even before they leave home. Children of our generation had their own particular set of challenges, but with or without parents at our side, we are much less likely to see children and or families attending Sunday services today than in yesteryear.

Except for our baptisms, special events, or funerals, I do not recall regular church attendance by our family. As we got older and Mom earned her license to drive, things changed for the better in somewhat surprising ways that I will delve into very shortly.

Dad worked at least two jobs and was probably glad to actually have one day of real rest, so he skipped church for many years. On Saturdays he spent the better part of the morning and early afternoon cultivating his flowers and plants or manicuring our lawn. He'd enjoy a well-deserved break basking in the gentle breezes under the canopy of one of the ubiquitous aging oaks surrounding our yard. Pops had a gift for transforming a cutting into petals of flowers fit for a princes or a drooping seedling into a thing of beauty. This gift landed him the residential beautification award from the city of Daytona Beach.

I can "smell" the rich fragrance of the Confederate jasmine profusely covering the north gate, the fragrant aroma of grapefruit and orange blossoms out back, the deep pink rose bush at the corner of the front sidewalk, and the artistry of the salvia, petunia, zinnia, and hibiscus artfully arranged in our front yard. He would eventually come inside to watch a baseball game during spring and summers after he was satisfied with his pride outside.

Pops constructed his own bar-b-que pit under an umbrella of oak and pine trees in the northeast corner of our back-yard. That pit poured out aromas from chicken and ribs on many an occasional Saturday. Mom made a sauce especially for the meat, which Pops described as "the best," and it was! I think honey was one of her secret ingredients. I never saw Mom measure anything, but her stirring and occasional tasting netted a special sauce that always tasted the same.

Whenever we captured the perfect combination of ingredients for anything we had "concocted," Dad would say without fail, "Now make it the exact same way every time. Don't change nothin'."

On Sundays he read the paper, watched news programs, and later "hunkered down" in his favorite chair for afternoons and evenings of sports, especially baseball and football.

Our parents made every effort to attend school activities; science fairs, track meets, plays, football games or club inductions. Most of our teachers knew our parents and they them. Some of my fondest memories included travels with my parents and sisters to my brother Charles' high school and college football games in the late 60's and early 70's. Those Friday and Saturday games were full of excitement, energy and drama unlike any other. We all had fun supporting our brother and his teams, the Father Lopez "Green Waves" and the University of Tampa "Spartans".

During our college years, particularly those of mine and my sisters, Pops "never-really-new" but always dependable vehicle found its way up 95N to I-10 or 441 to Tallahassee or Gainesville. An ardent sports fan, he sacrificed some of his precious "days of rest" in front of the television, as well as a few dollars on speeding tickets to drive us back to "Noles" or Gator country. Pat and I never had cars in college and neither did Laura until her junior year. We traveled via Greyhound or Trailways Bus or occasionally with friends and acquaintances going our way. For all of those beginning and ending semester, quarterly or holiday trips to and from school, thank you, Pops.

Everyone was at Pops beckon call; he hardly ever answered the phone because as he once pronounced, "I don't get no calls." And neither did he answer the door. Pops lived as a "king," especially on Sundays, and in some ways personified what an ideal "day of rest" looked like.

We had the option of remaining at church after Sunday school or going home, in which case my brothers often chose the latter. Mom tried to attend as often as she could, but I don't remember whether or not my dad dropped her off, and I don't remember Mom or any of us walking home from church either. It's all somewhat of a "blur." Mom did not get her driver's license until I was in high school, so maybe by then she was driving us to Sunday school and church. Two of my three older brothers were off to college, never to live at home again, and the third of my eldest, who was at that time attending a Catholic high school, was studying Catholicism.

Mom's regrets about Sunday service attendance remained with her all of her days, but a life-altering event began to take shape in her life which proved much more consequential than those regrets ever would. Some who are reading this may not understand the depths of what I am about to reveal. Scripture states clearly that spiritual matters are "foolishness" to the natural man (I Corinthians 2: 11- 15). Needless to say, Mom underwent a spiritual re-awakening during the mid to late eighties and early nineties, which changed the course of her life forever. By then my siblings and I were well into our thirties and forties, and Mom was attending church regularly and participating fully in various capacities.

In the late eighties, my father decided to "join the church," which is the Baptist tradition of actually taking steps to become a member of the local congregation we attended at that time. One joined the church either by letter or on Christian experience or Baptism; Dad joined on Christian experience. He began attending regularly and participated in the business as well as the activities of the church. While Dad was enjoying his new-found involvement in our church, Mom was realizing a "newness" of life in Christ that I did not understand and neither did my father. One of my younger sisters introduced this concept for lack of a better word to Mom and me in the early eighties but none of what she tried desperately to explain or share made any sense at the time. We had been immersed in the traditions of the church in which we were reared but void of a genuine relationship with our Lord and Savior and hardly knew any of His word. I cannot speak for Mom, but my prayer life and intentional devotion to His service was as far from me as the state of Alaska. I lived in Florida.

For years, we practiced our religion in the manner in which we had been taught; we attended, paid our dues (not necessarily our tithes and offerings), and followed the by-laws of the church, not necessarily the mandates of the Bible. We listened respectfully and reverently to the sermon or speech but not necessarily a Bible-based message of hope and transformation. Oh, yes, there was always a scriptural reference, but the messages did not always teach the deeper meaning of salvation, sanctification, repentance, renewal, healing, and victorious living.

The renewal Mom experienced motivated her to heighten her prayer life as well as her personal devotional time, which included praise, worship, and prayer. As her devotional life became more solidified, the Holy Spirit gave her a hunger and thirst for God's word as well as a discernment for the true and unadulterated word of God. Unlike what I had witnessed as a child and young adult, Mom was anxious to go and hear the "word" being preached and more importantly taught. She was excited about going to church as well as Bible study and experiencing the love of God through open and more demonstrable praise and worship, out-reach, and missions, unlike her experiences in the more traditional churches we were used to.

My dad was truly baffled not so much by Mom's renewed devotional time and enthusiasm for worship but the fact that it caused her to attend more "word" services outside of the traditional church in which we were reared. And while she was elated that Dad was attending church as never before, she had to endure the sting of his criticism as to why she wanted to attend other churches (one in particular), which he viewed as disloyal. She knew that he would not understand this new-found spirituality considering his level of spiritual growth at the time, but she was able to cover him and our family in prayer more than ever before. He thought that our church was just fine, and in a way he believed that since he had decided to attend more regularly, he felt abandoned and maybe even betrayed when Mom began attending elsewhere. It was a sore spot, especially amongst my parents and myself as I was the only one of my siblings living in Daytona at the time. Just as Dad decides to become an active member of our family church, we are beginning to go elsewhere for heightened spiritual growth and development. He was not comfortable with that at all. But again, in fairness to my dad, he simply did not understand.

Mom, however, never ceased attending church with my father; gratefully she found a word, worship, and praise church commencing at an earlier hour, which allowed her to return home and join my father, so that they could attend their home church together.

Mom invited him to attend the earlier services with her often enough, but he always declared, "I'm going to my church!"

Her new life in Christ did not erase her regret about our family's failure to worship together, but it did teach her how to pray for our soul's salvation as well as for our safety and security on a daily basis. She knew she could not undo or re-do the past, but she was able to walk into the future with an assurance that her family was covered in the "Blood" and that one day we, too, would grow into the newness she had joyously and gratefully come to know.

During the last years of my dad's life, I witnessed a softer, more concerned, and compassionate side of him. That softer side was always there, but it was more palpable during those latter years. He always exhibited a rather tough veneer, but we all caught glimpses of just the opposite from time to time and on many occasions before his illness.

When chronic illness rendered him unable to live at home, he became a resident of the memorial veteran's nursing home. He lived there a total of forty-eight non-consecutive months mustering enough strength of will as well as improved health to return home on at least two occasions, one for a year and another for several months. In July of 2009, Pops returned to the nursing home for the second time where he lived until passing in November 2012.

Before he lost his ability to walk, he assumed the responsibility of escorting one of his buddies from their meal table back to his room. I once offered to do it myself, but Dad promptly grasped the curves of the wheelchair's handles and proudly proceeded to escort Mr. Mitchell back to his room. As the three of us made our way out of the dining room through the television viewing area and down the long hall to their rooms, it was clear that Dad relished the opportunity to be of service to his friend, and I basked in the joy of being a witness to it.

It was a late Indian summer morning, and Dad and I were sitting outside near one of the picnic tables at the VA. He was in a wheelchair by now as he had gradually lost much of the use of his feet and hands due to Parkinson's disease. Having brought one of my books of meditation, I began reading aloud the meditation for that day as well as the accompanying scripture. I knew by then that Dad was saved as I had ministered to him a year or two prior, so studying the scripture and meditating on his word was perfectly alright with him. By the way, my father had a multitude of health problems, but he never lost clarity of mind.

As I pondered the time frame of this particular visit with Dad's entrance to hospice care, it happened that the scripture we were studying was Psalm 91: 1-16 and the topic was Live Free From Fear. My visit was the Tuesday before he entered hospice. I read the meditative words and the accompanying scripture, and as we discussed the reasons God says we shouldn't fear, I casually remember mentioning harboring certain fears. Not prepared for the question from my father that followed, I remember that he didn't appear to be as engaged as he actually was, thus my surprise.

My father looked up from a partially held down head and asked, "What are you afraid of?" The look on his face was one of surprise and fatherly concern. I found a way to avoid sharing my fears and sparing him added anxiety for obvious reasons. His query was gratifying and fulfilling as somewhere deep within my spirit I believe that he knew I had nothing to fear based upon the words we had just read and that he truly understood it as well, deep down in his own.

As I matured and life invariably happened as they say, I allowed myself to see more of the personhood of my father than in my earlier years when we seemed more at odds than anything else. There were moments when the depths of his soul shined through and nuances of kindness and compassion were more evident. Yes, he was difficult more often than not, but scripture teaches us to look beyond each other's faults and see the need just as Jesus modeled with us.

Though "Nick" and Nettie were uniquely different in their approach to life and child rearing, there is one moment of solidarity in particular that I witnessed up close and personal and which has remained with me through the years. Needless to say, every parent knows the heartache that comes when consoling a child you love more than life itself. No parent wants to see us hurting and will do almost anything to take our pain away.

My father was sitting in his usual chair at the head of the dining table, but the chair was facing the kitchen; his shoulders slumped and both hands cupped his forehead. Mom sitting similarly but opposite him. It was clear that they were very sad and most probably had been crying. Dad looked up at me as I spoke coming in. Mom uttered a pained but always cheery greeting, no matter the circumstances as she tried hard to be brave. There were other times when I had seen them emotionally drained or sad, but for some reason, this time touched me more than any other. It showed me just how much they loved us and how wounded children, be it physically, emotionally, psychologically, or otherwise never escape the all-encompassing love of parents regardless of our age. Most will move heaven and earth to prevent us from hurting and even more to take the hurt away. My parent's hearts were "walking around" outside of their bodies that day because one of us was hurting and so were they.

Mom realized what was really most important, especially as she approached her most senior years. Yes, she firmly believed in family worship and that sound biblical instruction both solidifies and facilitates it. But she also believed in the work of the "scattered" church as well as the "gathered" church. That our intent should be to serve God by serving others outside of its walls; giving cheerfully of our time, talent, and finances, devoting time to God in prayer, praise, and worship and by diligently studying His word. Given the limitations imposed upon the gathered church due to the pandemic, it does appear that the work of the scattered church is even more relevant today. She did these things with joy and enthusiasm and with an unwavering faith that served and comforted her until the end. I truly believe that Mom would say that by far this was one of the most consequential of lessons not that she necessarily taught us but that she herself learned.

EPILOGUE

Just a few more values our parents employed to help further our development:

1. Provided unconditional "tough love." Yes, they loved us, and in addition, they also made us mind (obey)!

2. Repeated themselves. Telling us something one time was not enough. They repeated themselves. Get it?

3. Taught us how to "live" anywhere. Mama always said to us when we balked at her instructions, "I'm rearing you for the world, not just for me and your daddy."

4. When we failed to heed their admonitions, they responded with, "The world will teach you," and we were reminded that the world's consequences would be tougher than theirs.

5. Tried to rear us, so that if anything were to happen to them, someone might want to take us in. They stressed good manners and tried their best to re-enforce and encourage good behavior. Well-mannered children were more likely to be welcomed into others' homes.

6. Addressed even the most inconsequential or seemingly innocent things. We didn't get away with much of anything!

7. Continued to nurture and show active concern for us whether we were at home or abroad. They never shipped us out of their hearts just because we were old enough to be out on our own.

8. Mama ALWAYS told us that we were BEAUTIFUL and BRILLIANT. Yes she did.

9. Provided us as much exposure to cultural, civic, and social affairs as they were able to do so.

10. Our Pops always reminded us that "Time don't wait on no man." Mom always said, "Make hay while the sun shines." Get it done while you can and as soon as you can.

Questions for the Round Table

1. The author's mother was adamant about the impropriety of going to someone's home or attending an invitation only event without an invitation. Can you think of other reasons not stated in the book when these actions might be problematic?

2. Based upon your personal experience or those of others you know, discuss how having only one bathroom in the home might prove challenging?

3. What "creative" adjustments were made to help ameliorate the situation?

4. Almost everyone has a "shoe" story. What's yours?

5. Share an inspiring story concerning an elderly relative which affected or affects your life to this day.

6. The author writes that her mother was passionate about education almost to a fault; in what ways could her positive views be perceived as negative?

7. In addition to an academic college degree, list and discuss other ways in which people can become educated.

8. Who makes most of the decisions about money in your family? What would you do differently if you were in charge? Who most influenced your feelings about money?

9. Why are people more willing to wear a pair of glasses than a hearing aid? Do you think that vision is viewed as more important than hearing, and if so, why?

10. In the introduction, the author draws a sharp contrast between the way her father and mother viewed discipline. Is one method more effective than the other or does it depend upon the situation?

11. What does tough love really mean to you?

12. Was there ever a time when you felt you were paid a compliment that was not sincere? Discuss how a compliment offered "in season" can positively affect someone. Share a story that you are familiar with where a compliment proved life-giving or life-saving either emotionally, psychologically, or academically.

13. What role did/ does religion play in your development? The author shares re-collections about Sunday worship services from her parents' perspective. Which is more consequential, regular worship attendance or nurturing a personal relationship with the Lord? Explain how might they work in concert with each other?

14. Ponder the practical lessons you were taught which influenced you most.

15. What does it mean to leave things better than when you found them? Discuss a time when you visited friends or family and your presence made a difference in their lives. If you could either host or visit anyone in the world who would it be and why?

16. Which of the author's lessons were completely new to you? Which will you now incorporate in the life of your family?

17. Contrasts how you would phone or text your friends as opposed to the grandparent/s of your friends. Discuss whether titles, such as Mr. /Mrs., Professor, Doctor, and Pastor if applicable are appropriate at all/some of the time.

18. Discuss your thinking about gender equality and whether your opinions influence the way in which you interact with the opposite sex.

19. When calling the home of a married couple, why did the author advise speaking to 'the wife' first when making inquiries over the phone?

20. The author's father put a premium on truth. How much did having lived through the Great Depression, "Jim Crow," serving in WWII and experiencing the modern civil rights movement make truth non-negotiable?

21. Which of these 'practical wisdoms' seem obsolete? Which are most enduring?

22. As it pertains to the African-American experience both historically and more recently during the dawn of the modern civil rights movement, how would the way in which one speaks or presents himself have any bearing on others' perception of her/him?

23. Why does it appear people are more reluctant to confront a hearing impediment than a visual one?

24. If you were a parent, which of the "practical wisdoms" would be most difficult to teach, and if a child, the hardest to embrace?

25. Provide examples of when a text, email, or phone message was mis-interpreted, or mis-communicated to you or others you know. What was the outcome?

ABOUT THE AUTHOR

Helen Ryan Miles enjoys reading autobiographies and political commentary. On occasion, her opinions appear as reader's editorials in her local newspaper. She likes working puzzles as well as attending fairs and festivals. In recent years, her passion for beautification in both public and private spaces has re-awakened, having once served with her mother on the local community development board of her city. She was active in her church's feeding program (We Feed) and for many years the liaison between the Hope Fellowship Church (Daytona Beach) food pantry, local grocers, and Second Harvest Food Bank. Years of service as classroom teacher and school social worker have afforded her unique perspectives with regard to the academic and social needs of children and young adults. Miles is the author of two other books, Our Best and Most Accomplished, and Cotton-Candy Hair.

47593CB00017B/1056